Footprint of an Elephant

Footprint of an Elephant

49 poems

A.N. Persaud

 www.trafford.com

North America & international
toll-free: 1 888 232 4444 (USA & Canada)
phone: 250 383 6864 ♦ fax: 812 355 4082

Contents

Who says my poems are poems?
These poems are not poems.
When you can understand this,
Then we can begin to speak of poetry.
(*Taigu Ryokan*)

Whenever your spirit wants to speak in images, pay heed;
for this is when your virtue has its origin and beginning.
(*Friedrich Wilhelm Nietzsche*)

BOOK 1

AWAKENING

The Bridge

I came to an old bridge on my path.
Above the entranceway to the bridge hung a sign.
It was an ancient sign,
A message from the ancestors, already thousands of years old when
it was hung.

It said
"This is a bridge.
Do not build your home here."
A message in plain view for all to see
Who dare cast their gaze upwards
Away, for one short moment, from the dirt which covers the way

I try every day as I cross the bridge
To heed the message of those wise men and women
Who belong not to the past, but to the future
Because they did not make their home upon a bridge
But found their true abode upon the motionless foundations.

I strive to follow their examples.
I strive to remember, as I cross
        that this is a bridge.
This is a bridge, I tell myself, this is a bridge.
And I walk.

This is a bridge, a tool, a means, an implement.
But sometimes my body becomes tired
And it wants to stop and make a home upon this bridge.
But if I listen to this body, so attached to the bridge, and stop
It will be so difficult to rise and walk again.

I cannot stop.
Stopping and resting in the comfort of the known means a death.
The Memory will fade and I will not know that this is a bridge.

A.N. Persaud

I will mistake it for a home and greater beings will look upon me,
Poor creature, in pity.

I will forget that there is a destination,
Ends for which the means have been prepared.
I will forget what it is to walk
So I do not stop, even if the body complains.
And for the moment, even if it means that I stumble upon the bridge,
I keep my eyes fixed upwards and forwards
Knowing, in my heart of hearts, what I have always known
That this, what other men call life, is but a bridge.

One freedom

For that now which fades
Into the dream of a loss
Was never yours and could go
In a blink at Kipling's pitch and toss

At the cradle it was not
And neither in the grave
And for what is in between
Much does not belong, save

A drop into an ocean
The quickest of a blink
The weight of Maat's feather
The heart, it must not sink

So what provides the weight
Where there ought be none
Where what belongs and what stays on
Gives a deed not done

For here the heart will be without
The wings with which to fly
And those who come with hate to bear
Will knock you far from nigh

For hate will you return
And draw the dark side close
And though the hope will still stay close
The heart will beat morose

But this was never yours at start
Not at inception's peak
It is the mind which through time
Can make you strong or weak

A.N. Persaud

Of that which you cannot hold
Of that which you never held
Let go with the hold of mind
Stand up and be not felled

It will not come to bear
As meaning in the distance
But as a fork in the road
Paper doors in this instance

So with your fear, walk with force
The serpents hold no sway
There is but one freedom
Along the rocky way.

What begins as a seed

For what begins as a seed
Is written in the stars
What appears as many branches
Is a root that takes us far

The root, like the branch
Is plural in the form
And what they hold in high regard
Will emit from their scorn

And they who appear to hold us
Very far from our goal
Will be the very driving force
That makes a bird of the soul

For what starts as a simple step
The glory of the now
Is known by the masters
At whose feet our impulse bows

And so when I took your hand
When the heart would dictate word
The body could not follow
Still the movement not untoward

But that which moved
Was known not by the hand
But by an inner sate
Gentle, but knowing grand

And so your hand also moved
And your heart received the word
Which flew as if by magic
Through an unseen chord

A.N. Persaud

But the body was well witnessed
Seen through the unseen world
And so we took a second step
Like the sand toward the pearl

Now we stand in the midst
Of the next phase of the making
That which is not ours
And is never for the taking

Ram out of Ayodhya

What price is paid
When time delayed
What of life we would have made
If only we had stayed

But to stay a course
Of great remorse
When already the mind by wilful force
Has long departed the court

Like Rama out of Ayodhya
The deed was all but done
Before Ram's feet hit the street
The mind set all under the sun

And to him who will impede the motion
Of the will of mind
Will find his course intersect with a web
And receive his own in-kind

The wise will lay down their course
With the fabric of the mind
And when upon encountering a web
Will see the path sublime

For what appears the longest road
Fraught with unknown plight
Will prove itself the most efficient
A way to brighter light

Though the day be long and dark
The forest filled with fear
The land will be our guide and friend
And will enlist in our service a seer

A.N. Persaud

So we take the long, dark road
Narrow in its scope
But in its wake, freedom lays
And Sita's last great hope

When fools decide to tread

When fools decide, on paths to tread
Meant not for the foolish
Work and due and vision true
Are taken then by wish

And the fools who will now tread
On a path not theirs
Do so with much anticipation
But without the requisite care

And though they would not see reaction
Reaction would see them
And though they dream of being free
Karma becomes the pen

They will now enclose themselves
Each day a little more
Searching still for freedom
But each day digging hole

That which they long yearned for
Becomes now the disdained
Where they would on their own once walk
Now stand in need of cane

For being placed on pedestal
Looking now more like cage
They cannot even with justice claim
That forward-moving rage

Having not moved from surface
Hades waits in hole
And having held beyond one's reach
Darken stands the soul.

A.N. Persaud

We too are human

We too are human
Beneath all the noise
Amidst the deafening quiet
We too yearn for joy

There is a presence in a heart
That is covered, hidden, lost
Though the eyes take in the motion
They are covered with the dust

But we too are human
Even deep within the cave
When all that shows is animal
There is still much to save

We too are human
Though the words will not break free
It is only with the heart
That those with vision see

That we too are human
Though the race is not to us
We have not even entered
And shall not see the dusk

Each hour for us is a dawn
And we hope not to stay
There is a mountain to be climbed
For a movement into day

To be an actor in a stadium
In the midday sun
Is not a hope for those who
Cannot begin to hear the drum

For the march begins not at dawn
But well into the time
And if our brothers will not walk with us
We will walk with swine

But remember that we too are human
Though our tools be broken
When we walk upon the stage
We offer but a token

And what one can offer
Is nothing to the eye
That can see the collectivity
Together raise it high

Each soul can find a place
Of meaning and content
Even in a jungle
Is the message sent

To we who are human
Though it is hard to see
We send a plea, a silent call
For the hidden humanity

That we too are human
And we are your charge
This is a culture's judgment
But the load need not be large

So in this cave which is our home
We neither hear nor see
And in that you see us
There is no need for plea.

A.N. Persaud

A thing diminished

What becomes of a thing diminished
Its place in time and space
Its mark upon the order
Its need to go with haste?

And will I be present to a thing of value
On someone's relative scale? For value is
Conferred by the eye that beholds the small,
Steady steps of a tiny bird prancing upon
Mulched greenery. Those eyes then will also
See the flight, won through hard struggle,
Of that tiny bird – a flight not witnessed
By all, especially not those who look upon
The same landscape with indifferent eyes.
Those eyes able to penetrate the invisible
Will see value.

Let us then do away with the scale. Or
Keep it, at best, as a pleasant curiosity or
A satisfying intellectual pastime. And let
Me then penetrate the visible and enter into
This realm of causes, where the seed of worth
First buds.

And the eyes of those present
Will see tiny buds spring forth,
For being present will then be
Not about being *at*, but being *in*.

And the route within a thing,
An object, an event – the route
Is the same for them all.
It is to invest the human being *within*.

You came to me

You came to me, not near day's end
Unbent as in the past
The hate it seethes with too much ease
The love is hard to grasp

The vanity and pride
Pull me to the dark
And though I know I should let go
Long have I left Park

For anger drives, know reprise
The beginnings lay the course
And that life that once dreamt us
Now dreams us with a force

But to walk along the way
Is different than the knowing
And that which we would reap
Need be good for the sowing

So I find my hand extended
As you rap the door
Knowing that to help you up
I need rise from the floor

And let go of the chains
That bind me to the wall
For in the cave of human darkness
Fault not gravity for the fall

For it is we who hold the chains
We the chains that tie
And when the blame we try to name
We start to live the lie

A.N. Persaud

Inevitable is the change
From chaos to the cosmos
And then the line to new time
That wants to draw us close

So feel the pull and know the need
To work to that which draws
And rest not where impediments lay
Until the will sets law

Stim

Health is not the body
Ill is not the mind
When a man in time persists
What is that he finds?

Cut without a knife
Stunted with idea
Separated from the start
The godly curse of Hera

With the bucket filled
And when the light is dimmed
Difficult is it to climb
But encouraged is the stim

We stim upon the matter
And consume in-fashion goods
Do not question, we are told
This is not a should

For if we dare to think
To reflect upon the matter
We implicate ourselves
And need, then, enter water

We need to dive right in
To make right the wrong
And then upon entering
To see the way is long.

A.N. Persaud

Prepare the ground

There once was a chain that, in one direction, linked
The man of today to the superman of yesterday.
And like Atlas, in between the Earth and the Sky,
But not really anywhere, in the other direction
Linked us to the new heroes for whom we
Prepare the ground.

And born in this Age, pedestals on either side
Of the present, our necks become strained, but
Only if we have seen the vestiges of this chain
And the work done, unheralded, to reconnect
That which was broken. So with difficulty,
I look to my Age, head leveled, feet planted and
Begin my work.

The soil is rich. It has the nourishment of death.
Dreams broke, eyes closed, heads bent in submission
Have made the soil ready for those who wish to
Plant the last good in Pandora's box and undo
That which has befallen us. The gardener plants
For the future.

He must, of necessity, look to the next season
And prepare today. The Age has provided the
Fertile soil. The seeds must now come.
Come they will from every direction. And the fruit
Of one generation will give rise to the next,
Until one day, the gardener long gone, there will be
A towering tree. And the eyes of his descendants, themselves
Gardeners of the last good, look to the tree, and the
Father holding closely his son, urges,
"Keep the link unbroken."

I wear your band

I wear your band from time to time
But always in my heart. It links me with
A past formed partly of memory, partly of
The memories of others, stories that I relish
In hearing, stories that bring always a smile. I sit
Silent, without input, wanting only to soak in the
Spirit of a time now gone in the great abyss of the past.

You are my giant and I, a child on your shoulders.
How else does a child see far ahead? How else does he
See into the infinite past and the infinite future?
I stand on your earth, the same fertile earth
Where a year or two ago [probably more like 50 years ago
For those taken with the use of calendars], with
Bent back and sweaty, salty skin, you planted your
Grains of rice. It is still my staple.

I wade into your water and breathe your air.
It is the mineral-rich water of the countryside, both bathwater and
Avenue of transportation for the small row boats
That carried hopes and dreams by the hundred.

I am lifted by your fire – that same old fire
That you were able to carry and, somehow,
Transmit – the only way that fire is transmitted,
From one lit torch to another capable of
Being lit and sustaining the heat and the light.

I look to the band upon my hand, indents
Upon my wrists from the double snake heads
And I, upon your shoulders, am strengthened.
I am able to stand on the fire of an idea
For those not yet born who will, one day,
Need to look to the past and envision their future.

A.N. Persaud

Where has transcendence gone?

Where has transcendence gone?
O yeah, there it is, down the street
In the treads of your decade-old
White-stitched, black suede All-Stars.

Nice shoes, coming apart at the seams,
Insides peeling away, a symbol of
Your life – shiny bars and new paint
Masking the anguish and emptiness
Built from years of conscious inaction

Funny, how the inside and the outside
Work in opposite ways, the Inner
Torn asunder from lack of life, lack of
Challenge, lack of vision to thrown oneself
Into stormy waters and swim; the Outer
Falling apart through much use, many
Years of stylish persistence, temporary
Shoes against the immovable concrete,
The inanimate object on the fields
Behind Scarborough Campus, giant trees
Looking down as young love breaks forth
From an angst filled Idealist without path.
So, Idealist, where has transcendence gone?

The idealist, heart heavy from want of change,
Sits, pensive and unsure. From the first days on
Those green fields, peripheries marked
With bright orange mesh fences and
Green-coloured iron posts to the current
Structures of organizational hierarchy devoid of colour,
He ponders. He is a child of the Age of Iron
And corruption is a sea. He longs for a way out.
But there is only one way – labour. He knows

He must work the Inner as Hephaestus fashions
Through fire in the deep recesses of his forge.

But fashion he must, though the fire will burn,
The mind will sting, the emotions will wax and wane,
The body will tire, and the way will seem dark and untrue.

And the mind will loosen its attachment, the shiny bars
Will not hold sway and he will see that those firm metal
Doors hinged to the bars were, all along, made of rice paper.

A.N. Persaud

A warmth in being near

There is a warmth in being near
That the corporeal cannot bring
It is a power of the three
That can make the voiceless sing

Fruit from seed will come concrete
In a land that once was barren
And even if we need not touch
The heart will bring a star in

From the first small root
To the bottom branch
Straight to the very ends
The top will point to march

This is not near the end
But the warmth of life
Like a bud in the Spring
Will take birth through the strife

And the warmth we feel from being near
Will endure with the distance
And that which we feel in spirit
Will be made in form and substance.

BOOK 2

UPRISING

10

When I look at the scarab
And its quest toward the light
Transformation of a rotting matter
Into that which gives us sight

I can look all around me
And hope is in everything I see
A hope that comes not from the power to have
But from the power to Be

And this power is one
Which seeks the light of truth
A light which does not shine on matter
But illuminates the ageless youth

For time and chance cannot touch that
Which a human heart has made
In this, the raising of a union
With effort each victory is paid

The battered warrior will walk the path
And fight each last fight
And pass through the *mayavic* day
To reach the starry night

We build our staircase to this heaven
With a pace not of this time
The years roll by like days and weeks
And forged are the ties that bind

For our hearts, my friends, have become bound
In ways we cannot understand
Like a traveling ship wary of the sea
Ever searching for its land

A.N. Persaud

A land that is the destiny
For souls that ever seek
For souls who 'til that very end
Will be working for the peak

And the years still roll on the hills of time
And the eyes still ever shine
Those eyes that see beyond the surface
Beyond the world of mine and thine

Those youthful eyes that saw a dream
in a barely visible seed
Did not discard the tiny offering
But planted with word and deed

And the fruit that will come in a season of bloom
Will be sweet beyond the dream
Its juice will quench the thirst of a people
A *karma* completely unseen

And so we forward along the way
Under the gaze of a daughter of life
In a space that's charged with a hint of magic
And with a joy from walking light

Tending our garden along the way
The seeds of light we sow
Knowing that through the next set of doors
Only that which is planted will grow

When you close the gate

When you close the gate to stop the flow
It enters through the cracks
And when you stand guard at the front
It enters through the back

When you turn it off at day
It comes on in the night
And when you do not want to hear
It bombards through the sight

When you stand up most firm
It knocks you to the ground
And when you face the right direction
It turns you back around

Power then slips from the hands
The body feels no force
The mind is weak without control
But still we stay the course

For when you start the forward way
Resistance there will be
It comes from the way itself
But its agents will you see

So when you see them on the way
Know them for what they are
To the time, they're karmic mimes
Your ticket to the stars

Use those agents of the way
As means and not as ends
They impel to paths and roads
That for which you were sent

A.N. Persaud

What lingers

What lingers on within the mind
Will give direction to the heart
And on a crooked, twisted way
There is little to the start

That all important time of impulse
Poisoned by the mind
Which sees the double rivers
But not the golden hind

For the subtle behind a cloud
Is difficult to see
For even in the sunlight
We must offer up a plea

It will be the eyes of children
That see behind the veil
And their plea will be the deed
Beyond the world of fail

So step with care, over there
Behind the golden hind
And ready yourself for the distance
The race will not be kind

Don't Look Back

Don't look back, the eyes do not see
That which they saw yesterday
The vision of that which has not been
Impedes the forward way

Now come early morn, when all doors are closed
Still solace does the soul ever seek
And while merit will be the end of a cycle
Redemption is not for the weak

For bliss must be conquered, arrows at target
Flying full force through the ether
The pace is a run, under blistering sun
Merit will not wait for weather

So short out the mind, bring the sublime
And the rocky way to the stars will you follow
For arrows are substance that tend to the distance
And en route puncture that which is hollow

And doors that are locked must first hear the knock
Of he who would here pass through
For the key is the mind, turning through time,
Which lock doors that cannot, of existence, pass proof

Don't look back, the eyes cannot see
Obstacles that do not exist
The eyes must follow each shot arrow
To that on which the soul must subsist

A.N. Persaud

Throw yourself

Like a red wooden bridge
Over a creek
Like the unnamed hero
Who is still on the seek

You stretch your hand
And offer up your strength
I must, for the time, say no
The thirst yet to be quenched

But it is a healthy thirst
The yearn to reach and give
I look into your eyes, my child
And see the will to live

And what is life to you, my child
It is to throw yourself
To step foot in the Rivers Two
To draw One Life from the well

There is a joy from living deep,
A life drawn from the core
A life that does not know the false
Like the eagle, whose end is to soar

Like that eagle throws itself
Into rocky cliff
It is to live at the speed
Of ever asking If

And when the smile within the eyes
Fades from dread fatigue
Know that you, like me, my son
Must fight the dreaded weed

We must fight and kill the small,
The petty and the narrow
To know exactly where to thrown
And to wheel them on the barrows

Once that fight begins, my child
It will not end on land
Remember trying to disentangle
Those thousand grains of sand

A.N. Persaud

Balloons

Like bars of gold to me
Balloons up in the air
And what to artifice deemed unworthy
To perception, kingly fare

Come the granted value
Via the joy of ends
Like Theseus on a journey
To the centre for amends

Like Ludo on a human scale
The journey's not in things
But from a point of origin
Home we come again

Balloons up in the air
It is the journey home
And though we see collectivity
The journey's made alone

For it cuts a path
Straight into the heart
And each time that we fall
We see another start

To kill dead the Minotaur
Is not about possession
It is an act of the Being
No floccinaucinihilipilification

Balloons up in the air
Persona has come to school
To learn from the Master
The function of the tool

Like bars of gold, the cage is held
In very high esteem
Yet with slight breeze through open window
Begins the undoing at the seams

For that which glitters on the path
Is not merit of the time
It is another serpent coiled
If in the field of mine

Like balloons up in the air
Short lived but flying high
We aim to live, not to last
And we to the distance tie

A.N. Persaud

Open the windows

Open the windows, gaze outside
Look toward the skies
Open the windows, let the air
Sweep away the lies

That have held you in your stead
Breathe now new air in this room
That is at once comfort and death
At once a window and a womb

You cannot stay in small confines
For it will mean the death
Of that which has just begun to bud
How then to face a threat?

Open the windows, look beyond
The narrow confines of your square
Garments new are possible
Beyond that which well you wear

Make way for the vantage new
Now that the blinds are gone
Hear the words sung anew
From that old, familiar song

But when there is no song to hear
No one to play the tune
No conductor in the house
Do pick up the broom

Prepare the house for the master
Make the clarion call
Stand up from the floor, apprentice
Stand up and be tall

So that he from up high
When looking down may see
Hands reach up from the depths
Conductor, it is we

Waiting to play under a master
Orchestrating harmony
Instruments are readied
Of purpose, clarity

So apprentice, open the windows
Sweep today these floors
The toil we toil on this day
Will tomorrow be lore

A.N. Persaud

Stand among the young

In that dark night born from light
As life from the death
And from those first steps, oft repeated
Is life born from the breath

For even in the darkest night
Is light's seed alive
And in those terrible battles dark
We battle for the five

That race of man who will come
From somewhere in the present
Will be born in the dark
From that which currently isn't

As fear is to the fearful
So love to the lover
And we draw near that which we fear
And all else by it covered

This is why the resistance must
Be born in this fall
For whatever the state of the weapons
Clear is the clarion call

The fall begins in the man
Who does not stand erect
He who once fought for good
Will fully fall the fête

While he who stood steadfast
In times good and bad
Will once again stand among
The young and be fully clad

For in that tower of darkness
The fallen now stand tall
But on such dark support
That inexorable the fall

A.N. Persaud

A room for music

What life is this that we live
It is the life we know
And if we live it well today
It will serve the morrow

For though we struggle, each of us
With quotidian task
Each of us strives for more
Inclining to that which lasts

Through performance and perfection
Of that daily duty
We slowly approach what lies beyond
Linking time with song and story

And at the end of a work
With ceremony mark the time
The glory of the struggle
That we will not fall in line

For the crooked marks with form
Disguising disingenuous ends
And for all that we do each day
We will do all but bend

We will not be broken
Though your stick be strong
We will not bend from the Right
Though you push the wrong

And even if we cannot say
For sure what is the Right
We know that what you push
Is unthought, ill-formed might

So we walk, head up high
Sure of what we feel
Add to that intelligence too
Intuition of the real

So we push back everyday
For that which will one day be
Care with every step
Know now we will not flee!

A.N. Persaud

The cradle in the labyrinth

The cradle of the future
In younger arms than those
Who will one day look beyond
To see the future's throw

In arms that once raised themselves
Appealing with upward gaze
Stand now at the ready
At the entrance to this maze

But a maze does not circle
To the centre of the heart
And in the labyrinth now he stands
Walking in the dark

For it is the darkness
Which will one day lead to light
Just as the time of peace
Will one day lead to fight

It is the warrior who must
Conquer gross duality
And see that the tiny seed
Is nothing but the tree

That which we envision
Has its place in space
Where once carried the walkers
Now they set the pace

Sawol's brood

There once was a time
When dreams were hidden well
When the land was inundated
And a task upon me fell

From beginning did I fail
To step foot in the water
To reach out with a hand
To Sawol's only daughter

And daily did this plague my mind
Undisciplined as it was
The failure to make truth known
Great fear was the cause

And for years did I battle
This dis-ease of the mind
Until there was remedy
I thank the goddess Time

For it was no strength of my own
But a collapse of the system
All landmarks ceased to be
Of need the path turned within

And so the daughter of Sawol
Followed not her father
But descended smooth terrain
To touch the unwarmed matter

And I who turned within
On the path of no retreat
Struggled a rocky way
And nowhere found a seat

A.N. Persaud

Movement remained requisite
For those who chose this way
Navigating without aid
When Sawol's voice would say

Follow the call you hear, my child
Let not emotion intrude
Keep company with those on the rocky road
Stay close to this brood

The chariot

You see me now from very far
And what must you think of me
Disillusioned and disenchanted
I see modernity

But unable to rise quickly from the fall, I linger
Looking at the blood on the gray, cracking pavement.
Having not expected the fall, and being told always
To rise, with difficulty, I conceive lifting myself.

It is not my body that feels injury, but the
Small ego, attached to an image, a mask that
For too long have I worn, forlorn.
It is *persona*, the mask covering newborn truths,
Scarce expressing them. And here, now, naked I lay
In crisis, an opportunity for the eyes to turn inward.

But unaccustomed to the dim view, like going indoors
After being bathed in the midday sun, I see little and grope
Without landmark, hoping when only navigation will do.

And the pain, originating in the mind but felt throughout
The body, will be my chariot. It is necessary
That I drive it in to morrow, and perhaps then,
You and I both will think differently of me.

A.N. Persaud

Go not with a heavy heart

Go not with a heavy heart
Clear your bag of stones
Make clean the stables
Before you are but bones

Weigh on the scales of life
Who will remember you?
What deeds were done with spirit?
Which deeds were really true?

The heavy heart stays on Earth
There is no time of rest
Before the day our deeds are weighed
Let us not keep our best

Let us give it freely
Let us live as brothers
Let us say what needs to be
And let only appearance be smothered

Let us elevate, then
The golden words of old
Let us imagine in deed
The words we have been told

So often and so purely
From the lips of the wise
To stand within the Being
And eliminate the guise

Who?

When the night falls, when the time comes
When the hour of need is most desperate
Who will rise, who will stand tall
And who, among human beings,
Will prove themselves divine?

Who will make the gods look down and take
Notice that when most we needed an act of
Kindness, a hero stretched forth an arm and
Was carried beyond tiredness, not by the
Strength of his physical body, but by the
Well of virtue in his heart?

Who, beyond the cold din of rational reason
Will see that which is most needed to
Resurrect a humanity suffering from the
Great lack of Light in the world? Who will
Light a torch and shine that light upon the
Path that all have heard of but none ever seen?

Uprising

Part II

A.N. Persaud

Two heads rise: the battle for man

When morning comes and two heads rise
Each not so different than the other
Each from a different station
Taking babe from mother

For labour given to creation
Does not ownership convey
And that given to those of privilege
Is taken from the slave

For what makes free a man
Is to that which he belongs
We see not the caged bird
But hear the voice of song

And the slave is he who
Without cage, will still be attached
And after leaving circumstance
Cannot the past despatch

In he whose home is suffering
There lies a great discord
There is no balance in the force
To fight, he has no sword

His weapon, still unready
Is his living force
And there a dragon in his path
Though he is off the course

For the enemy will appear
In those moments most tense
It is not in the easiness
And there is no need for fence

But rather, come, embrace the fear
For hate is not an end
Hate will build a fence for you
But love alone can mend

For love alone can carry
A man away from hate
And if that child is born a slave
It is still he who makes his fate

So when the bright morn rises
Be I a free man or a slave
I know I rise, a man alive
And my home is not this cave

A.N. Persaud

Battle for the light we fear

Word brought forth as it is
A single ray shone through
A solitary candle lit
All contingent on the view

On perception and perspective
On seeing from atop
The higher that a man goes
The further can he drop

Especially when elevated
Without means or ends
When attachment stretches forth its fingers
When the road turns and bends

The mind will itself be bent
Necessitated by the thought
It must be bent before it's sent
To be made straight by the battle fought

And like any battle fought
One against the other
There will be pain, hands will be stained
In the mission to recover

That which is buried deep within
By many means and forces
It is to reach, its walls to breach
The life that ever courses

A great unease: death within

I felt a great unease
And reached for the Life
I did not hear reply
But felt only strife

It was the beginning
As all great things start
With a great big distress
That lives in the heart

For that heart is the motor
And the swamp is called Comfort
Where ease cannot drive
As healing born of hurt

So in this chaos that is life
I undertook a first step
Feet just on the field
As life from the death

But that first step was no walk
It was a leap of will
It was a leap into the battle
For birth comes from the kill

The death of the vice within
That a human voice could speak
A step at the very base
But still toward the peak

But into the battle grand
The battle raged with fire
Unable to tell friend from foe
Upliftment was the mire

A.N. Persaud

Thrown down to the ground below
Perspective run away
The base metal of the Alchemists
Served upon a tray

And being a novice in the art
I knew not what to do
I reached for the words of old
And atop a sword I drew

A sword for the kill
And a stilling of the mind
Duty proved difficult
But Duty would I find

Like an arrow to its target

Like an arrow to its target
Straight through a cloud of smoke
Like invader to the castle
Straight across the moat

I was to the light of Being
But felt it like the dark
I could not see my place
And appeared to leave no mark

Instead my head could not see straight
There I was laid bare
I could not feel inside of me
But from out, I felt the stare

Of those who would not know the path
And did not like the walker
Of those who dealt in pettiness
Heart kept within a locker

So in that state of weakness
Attacked from all around
Struggle did I to stand upright
With body to the ground

Like magnet to the pole
And love to the lover
Lies from the eyes not disguised
And words kept under cover

The weight of this gravity
Made this a walk of will
And though the downward pull is slowed
The mind is far from still

A.N. Persaud

A walk through the ring of silence
Where no other sound is heard
A deafness in the field of mind
The one freed from the herd

So now to the fire throw me
True direction to be sought
Out of the ease that kills
There is a battle to be fought

So take me to the field, my master
I know not where to search
I feel the cool wind at my back
And on the edge sit perched

Ready for the flight of will
On the wind of destiny
Ascent from the Year of Merit
With time's passage like a tree

One-way street

It used to be a two-way street
It used to appear complete

But the space has changed
Time has played her tricks
Indulgence will lose her way
Spontaneity run come quick!

Even thought the precipice
Will find us from time to time
I find myself being led
Above mine and thine

And then the road, once a choice
Becomes a one-way route
Therein lies an unfound freedom
For the music is Krishna's flute

It is the voice within that speaks
In times of dark and light
And a knowledge that the light
Will shine most bring at night

So even when the day looks dark
Scale the precipice
It is a road, but with one goal
Fight your way to bliss!

A.N. Persaud

Shall I let you sleep, my love?

Shall I let you sleep, my love?
You who bear my world
I now look and yesterday see
The woman from the girl

Shall I let you sleep, my love?
These silent acts you'll know
Heavy eyes wait for sun's rise
As the garden waits for hoe

Shall I let you sleep, my love?
And the call shall I heed
To do that which serves tomorrow
While today riding restless steed

Like Gilagamesh in search of death
And that which overcomes
I feel the need to fight dis-ease
Like a thousand burning suns

For that which is diseased
Look first in the mind
And like Gilgamesh you fight
Full out in broad daylight

But now it is the dark of night
And tonight you sleep, my love
For at the cry, your mother's eye
Will lift you back above

For it is the cry of need
That pulls you from your sleep
It is, in you, the call of Right
As quickly morning creeps

Shall I left you sleep, my love?
And do when no one sees
It is the only way my heart
Will drop me to my knees

For deed done right, day or night
Is far from spectacle's hour
It is because we need to reach
And when on the boat, we row

So, shall I let you sleep, my love?
Close your eyes tonight
For acts that serve the distance
Belong not to the sight

A.N. Persaud

Spit not the venom

Still, am I needed
By a world at war
Now that we see each other
From so very far

I had a dream in the night
And a message came to me
A message from the undisturbed
And the message was to be

To be oneself from that place
Where disruption cannot hold
To listen without thought of council
And let the story once more unfold

To listen with eyes on one bank
While the feet prepare to leap
And let the killer in the grass
Remain among the meek

For the word in image form
Was spit not the venom
And so it came, without disdain
Like rhythm without drum

Straight and sure, without the middle
No need for medium
A new voice to make more noise
On a road called Tedium

Spit not the venom, Dragon
Let the story be told
Let the snake sit and take
And bring an age of old

But spit not the venom
It will poison only the spitter
And any fruit from this root
Cannot be but bitter

A.N. Persaud

Fertile ground

The road that takes a man
In weather cold and harsh
Looking for a ground to walk
But leading to the marsh

By constant inundation
Is the land made fertile
And sweet will be the fruit
While bitter black the bile

And so the man around the
Marsh, will tread, eyes on the ground
And that which he hopes to lose
Will by the wheel be found

For the path elected
In avoidance of one's lot
Will see the tree of destiny
To the face be brought

And when the man within the sand
Unable to move or sway
Will find his freedom not on the ground
But in the light of day

The slowed pace

I walked with quickened pace, heading west
Sun in my eyes, bags in hand,
Sweat upon my skin. My eyes squinting
And body in discomfort, I turned south and slowed my pace.

I could now, not walking into the sun,
Look up and see with clarity. Bags
Still in hand, my body nevertheless, with a
Sense of relief, trod forth.

The slowed pace enabled vision of a
New landscape. Relief coupled with
Love and surety of path made
The same work seem as play.

Destination known, a detour, to the
Eyes of the rigid and extreme seemed a
Step out of *the* path, a betrayal of
Devotion.

But the path, ever made with the walker, is not ever false.

A.N. Persaud

Not a place to close one's eyes

This is not a place to close one's eyes
It is not a place to rest
It is not a place to break the vigil
For quick will come the death

This is a place to heed the call
It is a place to be upright
It is a place to lift the head
When others lack the sight

It is a place to see the devil
The devils, inside and out
The devil who will plant himself
And plant the seeds of doubt

It is a place, when others run
To be still in the mind
When others come and run you down
To stand up and be kind

It is a place and a time
That has been turned around
And when all others turn to the heavens
You must dig the ground

This is a place of mass appeal
A service to the stone
Scarce is the air or fire
Plenty is there to bemoan

So when all others flock
In service of the small
It is the time to fly alone
In honour of the tall

The grand and cyclopean
From beyond memory's reach
And when we say no words at all
It is then that we teach

A.N. Persaud

No obstacle prevails

On this path, no effort is lost
No obstacle prevails
No wind is disadvantage
To he who knows to sail

He who lives death, enjoys life most
Embraces the struggle and the toil
For under every flower
Look, the serpent coiled!

After the victory of the battle
Serenity is your lot
No serpent coiled will shake your toil
As you undo each knot

For the strength of he who will
Enjoy life the most
If untested is not known
And lives then like a ghost

So let each day be your last
Without unrest or slumber
Effort amidst the world of appearance
To hollow out the lumber

And with this log, we will set sail
At odds with the current to target
Driftwood in our path
We avoid it or we break it

Either way, it cannot stand
As prevailing reality
When the crew on hollowed log
Set their eyes to sea

The Sixth Labour

Like Heracles looking for those
Stymphalion birds well hidden
There is a dark, dense forest
That does not know our bidding

How can we fight and slay
That which we cannot see
For to the darkness of the forest
Our hidden enemies

And if we shoot without precision
Arrows to the waste
They cannot make their way
Past the forest face

So it is as I walk
Knowing not what to fight
But feeling the labour, far from a saviour
Yet to the blind, new sight

Thought the arrow can penetrate
Even the darkest day
This is the night, devoid of light
And even more are the birds here at bay

So hold for the moment your weapon
Use the mind and the sound truthfully
Sound from the ground, the birds come around
And now in the day try to flee

Pick up your weapon now, hero
Let fly the arrows of death
Now that the worst, in day writing verse
Has on the table Opportunity set

A.N. Persaud

So waste not a moment, come to the table
Here opportunity laid bare
Use every energy, killing the enemy
The beast that would kill you is fare

It was said

It was said that I could not meet the grade.
I, with some doubt, stood and looked to
The past. With ailing body, sweat dripping
And eyes fixed upon my movements, I reached
And gave that which was within.
I surpassed requirement with Life.

It was said that I would not be counted present.
I came through the purifying waters and
On bended knee, knelt before the standard
Of hope for a world not only new, but also
Better. And, with spirit, I gave.

It was said that I should not pass through
The door, and then it was closed to me.
After years of walking, I approached the
Gates to see them close just as the last
To gain entrance had passed through.
She had not walked, but, by her servants,
Was carried to the gates and ushered
Through on allegiance. I railed against
The injustice of the closure of the gates
To a worthy walker and at the unceremonious
Admission on mere favour to the sloth
and indulgence of modernity.

With my mind still struggling to loosen its firm
Grasp, my eyes began to look elsewhere,
For I have been told that, in life, when one
Door closes, another inexplicably and inexorably
Opens. So my eyes began to scan. There is to be
Yet more walking ahead, the direction of the path.

A.N. Persaud

And knowing that there are as many paths as there
Are walkers, I strive, with eyes open. And
Knowing also that it was said that I should not,
Without fail, I shall! I shall!

BOOK 3

CONQUEST

Risen

Risen from a time long gone
A time ever near
Risen from a hidden dwelling
By those who walk with fear

Go where there is fear, my brother
For therein lies a treasure
Go beyond the grasp of hand
Beyond the pain and pleasure

Any endeavour along the way
Worthy of the time
Belongs not to the moment
Is neither mine nor thine

So in those moments not known
By the experience of the mind
Must I find by the dimmest light
A window to the sky

A window from a small, closed space
In the limit of the known
The comfort of the agony
By that same hand was it sewn

But to rise above the limit
Is to acknowledge the tailor
And his work, the hand that stitched
The glove will also be the wearer

And as we lift each solid brick
To build the temple in and out
Each new lift will make us swift
And bring the inner work without

As the structure and the builder

A.N. Persaud

The two, they grow in tandem
The work from far, now near the bar
Becomes impossible to abandon

For now the two are one
Creator and creation
As the path being made with each bent glade
With every forward motion

So come the new upon the old
And the two together fashion
A work from time, of unknown design
Emanating from the passion

Kairos and the fire

I leapt into the unknown
Without much give to thought
I gave myself to Grand Design
But there was a battle to be fought

I was thrown into a fire
Each day I hoped for respite
But there is no rest for those on trial
And each day my mind said "test it"

So I suffered through the days
As those slow to learn will do
The nights were filled with Beauty
But those days led to the True

And then came Opportunity
Racing through the door
Looking more like fire
And said I, "some more"

I grabbed him by those locks
Before he passed this time
Less did I suffer
More did I refine

For once he passes out of reach
Opportunity looks not behind
He is not for those fond of sleep
But for those fond of the climb

And so I climbed, very slowly
But with steady beat
The movement is not anything
That one could call retreat

A.N. Persaud

Now I look ever upward
As we forward along the way
And the night still is a place of Beauty
Where the stars may lead to day

I've come to kill you, Mr. Persaud

I've come to kill you, Mr. Persaud
Fine. Which part of me shall die?
I've come to take you to the brink
To the other side

To that side and back for more
Through the window pane
We each look upon the other
And I know this is the game

I must kill this beast
Slay him without doubt
He must cease to be a beast
To bring myself about

I've come to kill you, Mr. Persaud
Fine. Let us engage in battle
Let the field of dharma shake
Let each warrior feel the rattle

When one engages in fight the beast
Who comes from hidden dwelling
It is a fight for the future
A battle for the telling

I've come to kill you, Mr. Persaud
To take that which is mine
Then let us cease the talking
And see who now shall die

This ground is consecrated
By high Ares kneeling
The Roman Mars, both see the wars
So let us get to dealing

A.N. Persaud

There is no half-way in this battle
Arjuna's not in the middle
The ground is red, unmade the bed
Here, no one hears the riddle

It is a noise that brings the silence
A sight which closes eyes
This is a battle which brings together
The disparate ties that bind

I've come to kill you, Mr. Persaud
To bring belonging home
Home is a place in the future, Beast
This is a place of to and fro

A place only of transience
Mistake it not for the real
Defend it if you must, Beast
My full force shall you feel

It is I who have come to kill you, Beast
We both shall die this night
So make the leap, come as you are
And let us start the fight

Now you hesitate, Beast
Now you've come to die
Now is the time to see the truth
But more so to see the lie

I have come to kill you, Beast
Through my love of peace
Let me open a flower
Let me lay a wreath

A crown upon the head
Of the victor shall it lay

And for every victory
There is a cost to pay

For he that rules the underground
Shall rule also the world above
And when the world deals in hate
You must deal only in love

Then only will the beast be slain
And stand the victor also changed
This will not be the one who saw the beast
But a warrior of new fame

He was a poet when this started
And a warrior now he stands
Ever at the ready
In possession of his land

A.N. Persaud

Disciples on trial

I see them all before my eyes
Disciples all on trial
The heart of the heart of the human being
On sojourn all this while

And when the heart of the human being
Is touched like never before
Perception gleans a mystery
Simple lives become a lore

Disciples who will walk
Strong against the wind
And in their heart, light a spark
Now see Master and friend

What once was disillusion
Resistance of the mind
Has slowly turned, the inward burn
The metal in the mine

Precious is perception
Mysterious is the matter
And that which starts upon the earth
Will then evolve to water

That ladder leading from
One element to the other
Like the hurt of giving birth
Like the child from the mother

And in the air shall they rise
The elephant black to white
For that which happens in the dark
Will one day face the light

Resistance is a teacher
To that very end
And that place beyond attachment,
Every wound, must mend

And now upon the beast
Subdued and turned around
Disciple, Guru, come as one
When the fire is found

A.N. Persaud

Merit

We make our Merit,
Not by time, chance or place,
But by that one thing.

Hunger, said Hesiod,
Goes with the work-shy man!
To work is to be an actor,
It is to struggle,
It is to forward upon the stage
Making efforts toward those
Unnamed, almost unknown ideas
That shine through time
And are not dimmed with its passing.

Those lights make bright the stage of our actions.
They enable us to not be afraid of time,
But make time afraid of us, pyramids!

Ahh, those pyramids, planted on the earth
But whose tips point always to far-away suns,
Even when we do not see their light.

Whose lights?

Whose lights are on
In this dark night?

A.N. Persaud

The Footprint of an Elephant

Like life in destruction's path
This is a causal game
The footprint of an elephant
Creation is not tame

It is a wild jump to naught
When we cannot see
A landing ground beneath the fog
That the mind would flee

But to run the other way
Fearful of the fall
Unaware of the birth
That comes from breaking walls

But to break a wall
That will not stand up long
Is to hold when others fold
To know there will be song

To know that which once was
Was of yesterday
Today knows a brand new form
It too will not stay

But with new form, each new line
Life's thread does not cease
The time goes by, but does not die
And what might have may still be

The undulating way

The feel of magic all around
I saw it in the morn
I saw the past in front of me
That same future newly born

It is at once the present
The future and the past
It lives in the unseen heart
But fragile like the glass

It can only be seen
Along the undulating way
By he who rides the elephant
And knows enough to say

The monkey who once pulled the beast
And left me far behind
With tools to pull and prod the beast
Ten steps from sublime

After those ten steady steps
About-face must we turn
Like coming back to cave
Again we feel the burn

But he who by the fire
Feels the need to reengage
It is a grace, not saving face
To free man from the cage

14

Sowing seeds on an arid land
One flower on the earth
What, with great difficulty
We laboured for the birth

Still we labour, for a movement
At conception does not end
There will be much to grow
And there is still much to mend

For all our matter is with us
At inception's spark
And for all that we labour
It is but a start

A beginning on a land
Appearing green and new
But there in the shadow
That demon I just slew

And in every crevice
Every corner, every little turn
Growth requires vigilance
For it is more than the heart that burns

Our land wakes and cries
And longs to use her soil
And for a being to come with tool
And on the land to toil

To toil with precision
To work and never stop
To paint a picture of the work
And build for the land a prop

A bridge to a land of flower
One of bursting bloom
This is a work of the distance
An End will not be soon

And so walking through these years
We have just begun
We plant a banner on the land
But the wheel has not yet spun

We move from point to point
And give with a heart of gold
And very slowly carve a niche
A story still untold

And carvers from across the land
See the work we do
Some will come to lend a hand
And some will join the crew

But our boat appears to row
Against the current of the time
Some will fear the movement
Toward the sublime

It is a movement that demands
An effort of its crew
And encountering a matter
With some discomfort too

But all of us, we suffer,
Those of the crew or not
But what result will come about
Will lay in what was sought

But results will not always show

A.N. Persaud

For the upstream rowing crew
And many oars will be broke
In service of the true

But we know of others
Further up the stream
And of the many obstacles
Between us and a dream

And so the crew, some to row
And some to till the land
All stand in service
Of a vision grand

And as we stand
Some will fall, lost along the way
But luminosity as an End
Is not a case of may

It is a case of will
Over impatience and betrayal
And of a crew who look ahead
And who will raise the sail

And sometimes it will appear
That we start anew
And that all is lost
But there is something in the crew

It is something untold
Something not yet born
Something not yet seen
Something not fully formed

But it has begun

Inception has had its mark
And when we look about
And only see the dark

We know the shadow cast
It is no sign of the time
Only a word to hold the mast
And faith to keep the climb

And so through the cycles two
With weary foot we ascend
But with eyes that hold the skies
On this land which now we tend